Healed Heart

Healed Heart

Lily Joy Isaac

LPH

LUMINARY PUBLISHING HOUSE

ISBN (Paperback):978-1-968972-14-1

ISBN (eBook):978-1-968972-15-8

Cover Design by Julsiji Julsiji.wordpress.com

LUMINARY PUBLISHING HOUSE

LILY JOY ISAAC

To those who've realised there's no such thing as too much,

but that it was just the wrong person.

To Jesus, who's healed my heart.

Table Of Contents

HEALED HEART

xi

Playlist

Cults - Gilded Lily

Lauren Daigle - Rescue

TV Girl - Lovers Rock

The Walters - I Love You So

The Beatles - Yesterday - Remastered 2009

The Beatles - In My Life - Remastered 2009

Cigarettes After Sex - Apocalypse

Beach House - Space Song

Noah Cyrus - July

Cults - Always Forever

Lana Del Rey - Happiness is a butterfly

Gigi Perez - Sometimes (Backwood)

Cullen - Roslyn

Clairo - Bubble Gum

Lord Huron - The Night We Met

Zeph - Forever & Always

Richy Mitch & The Coal Miners - Evergreen

Patrick Watson - Je te laisserai des mots

Mazzy Star - Fade Into You

Coldplay - Sparks

LILY JOY ISAAC

Billie Eilish - i love you

Chance Peña - In My Room

Cigarettes After Sex - Sunsetz

Dr. Dog - Where'd All the Time Go?

Beach House - Silver Soul

Lana Del Rey - Brooklyn Baby

Cigarettes After Sex - Sweet

Arctic Monkeys - Baby I'm Yours

José González - Heartbeats

Elton John - Your Song

Lou Reed - Perfect Day

The Velvet Underground - Pale Blue Eyes

Lou Reed - Walk On the Wild Side

AURORA - Runaway

Heart

Normality is a paved road: It's a comfortable walk,

but no flowers grow

– Vincent Gan Vogh

True Love

I knew you loved me,

When you sat down next to me beside a tree,

Handed me a red rose to proclaim your love,

It was like a special sign from above,

As if the heavens understood that all I ever needed, was your love,

Nicely dressed in a suit taking me to dinner, displaying your sense of fashion,

showed me that you have perfect passion,

I wore my favourite flowery dress,

In the hopes that you would be impressed,

You told me you'd grown the rose yourself,

Like the guys in the books on my bookshelf,

In the garden you'd built from scratch,

Not even Monty Don could meet your match,

When you showed me your garden,

At the sight of plants my hands which were once hardened,

Softened at your touch,

As we planted seeds together,

I hoped our flowers would continue to grow forever.

Rumours

Rumours are like lies which I beg to hide,

Wrapped in a box of diamonds as a disguise,

Carried from place to place,

Questioning weather, it's in the right space,

Are these truths or are they lies?

Long past the time they were crafted,

Many times, were they drafted,

Multiple versions of the same false accusations,

Giving me a bad reputation,

Yet I didn't do the same to you,

My comeback was overdue,

But I didn't step foot over the line of morality,

I cared for my rights and wrongs to have a form of accuracy,

The diamonds dazzle in the sunlight, their secrets hidden,

The truth bedridden,

Unable to express the reality of what their beauty hides,

Letting all their sharp sides slide,

Along your skin, through the layers,

Without the expectance of a betrayer.

Tears

Tears are the face to your trials and tribulations,

People are yet to see the strength you've shown,

Yet fast to notice how low you've flown,

The emotional release is bittersweet,

Like a wilted flower blooming once more,

As the broken petals fall after being torn,

Flying through the wind,

The negative emotions escape your mind,

And the tears run out of your eyes,

You begin to receive new revelations,

With old things becoming desolated,

As your eyes stop watering,

Your emotions stop faltering,

And you begin to make peace with past situations,

Which are no longer being shaken,

Allowing you to feel calm,

Away from any harm.

Cups

I spent time and effort creating my cup,

Carving the edges with precision,

And painting each part with perfection,

With oranges, purples, and pinks,

I put it up on display,

Proud of what I've made,

But then I begin to chip away pieces of my cup,

Giving away pieces little by little,

Until there's nothing left

Except a few pieces of broken clay.

I pour my time, energy and love into others,

Fixing everyone's cups while destroying my own.

When I finally decide to fix my own cup,

I regain a small part of my happiness,

Stop trading my own needs for approval,

I've learnt that no matter how kind, faithful or selfless I am,

I will always be enough.

Because in the end,

When silence fills the room,

And people walk out of the door,

I don't want to feel like a stranger to myself.

The Key

The key felt warm in my hand,

Its metal held more memories than my mind,

Slipping it into the old lock,

It hesitantly turns with a click,

And suddenly the door sighs open,

Light spilling across the entryway,

A spark of something sensitive stirs,

Breathing in the promise of what comes next,

Every shadow shrinking behind me,

The sky ahead is wide and clear,

And all my steps feel bright and near.

Growth

When plants don't grow,

You begin to look at the root of the problem,

Do you blame the leaves,

Or the environment?

You observe the soil and the sunlight,

Because that's what helps the plant.

When you aren't growing

You look around,

Is your environment good?

Will it help you,

Or do you need to go somewhere else,

To be able to,

Like you so desperately need.

The outside of a plant shows the world

What they want to see,

But the inside is filled with the truth

The stem shows the process,

And the time, which is taken,

For the plant to be strong and healthy.

We only show people what we want them to see,

But inside, the time it took is stored there,

And the situations that we went through,

To be who we are today.

As the flower is blown towards the light,

Its true beauty is revealed.

Feelings

Sometimes I want to scream and cry,

Let out the emotions we are unable to deny,

As fast as a light switch,

Wishing we could feel the numbness,

Like when the lights are off.

Until we realise,

That to heal, we must feel,

It's a slow process,

But one day our emotions

Will be ones of joy and happiness,

The laughter erupting from our lips,

Will not have been heard for a while,

And that's when we'll realise,

That our feelings have been healed.

Perfume

The presence of God is like perfume,

You feel it touch your skin when it's sprayed,

The scent brushes onto the tip of your nose,

You smell it all around you,

The scent encounters everyone,

In the same way that the Holy Spirit touches each person,

Like it did upon the disciples at Pentecost.

There are also many different scents

of the same brand of perfume,

In the same way that you can feel

the presence of God around you.

You love the precious moment when

you feel it for the first time,

And you can see when people are

an embodiment of Jesus Christ,

There are multiple ways that God speaks to us,

Perfume touches us,

In the same way that when God comes into our life,

He heals us.

War and Peace

I have become a soldier in battle,

Getting ready to fight, I put on my armour, clutching my sword,

Praying that I'll be safe and successful in this fight,

Yet as I come to face the opposition,

The person I see is myself.

I have been at war,

For far too long,

And all these bruises are worthless,

There's no need to go through these blind battles,

I should hand myself over,

To the one who wants to heal me

And I need to stop this war,

To have lifelong peace,

I must stop this battle,

And surrender to complete healing,

So that I'll be able to be a person filled with peace.

Many years after the battle,

The once blood-filled field,

Is now traced with greenery and growth,

It's lined with the beauty of the marigold flower,

The place is filled with yellows and greens,

Looking almost as peaceful as the sea.

2nd Chances

Society tells us to give second chances,

Then to leave completely

To protect your peace,

Because if someone isn't changing,

Then they simply don't deserve to be in your life,

But a good friend of mine says,

To continue giving people chances,

You don't have to cut someone off

To be creating boundaries,

You can distance yourself

without unfriending someone.

Forgiveness is like a tree,

Its leaves continue to fall

Until there are non left,

But then in a new season of life,

It gains new leaves,

When we don't show mercy

The times that we want to forgive,

Will decrease and eventually be almost none,

But with the grace of God,

We shall be able to forgive once more,

Society tells us to give second chances,

But God tells us to give unlimited chances

Because that's what he did for us,

He has given us more chances than we deserve,

So, we should do the same.

Red String Theory

When two souls are destined to be together,

They're connected by an invisible red string,

Like roots of a flower,

They're stretched out over centuries of space,

Yet they always meet at the bottom of the tree,

No matter the time space or situation,

They will always find one another,

It may get tangled, stretched, swirled or elongated,

Their souls are tied together,

Like branches which are at opposite ends,

Yet when rain falls, it shakes the leaves,

But they still stay strong,

This string connects soulmates,

Perhaps it's fate.

Candle

Once a candle is lit,

Its hot wax begins to melt

And it becomes a liquid,

Then after the flame has been blown out,

The white-dyed wax cools,

It goes hard once again,

And the next time the candle is lit

The process repeats.

Each time we suffer,

We go through many emotions,

But at the end of it all we have to heal,

It can be a slow or a long process,

The reason could be big or small,

But eventually we'll realise

Just like how the wax cools,

We will always be healing.

Paper

I started out as light and empty,

With space, which was plain and plenty,

It looked like I had stickers and stars

Placed over all my scars,

Rips and cuts, hidden beneath the scrunches,

Destroying my gut,

All the many punches,

I was told I was easy going,

Without any paper throwing,

Easy to use,

Without any misuse or abuse,

I was torn and creased,

Pieces of me misplaced,

As I went into unknown spaces,

But my paper was replaced,

As I unlearnt past mistakes,

The stars I once had became hearts,

And I was now lines with small pieces of art.

The Life of a Bee

When the other bees left the beehive,

Did you wish you could go out there and try to survive?

Collecting honey as if it's pockets of money,

Instead, you're stuck inside,

Forced to follow the rules of cycle and abide,

First you become a nurse, knowing your unable to disperse,

Then you begin to build the comb, getting closer to the freedom of your own,

Then you pick up your sword, standing guard to protect the hive,

Enabling other bees to thrive,

As your days are coming to an end,

You can finally escape into natures end,

Flying out to collect nectar,

Whilst staying in your sector,

You were able to stay strong, but at what cost,

When you were unable to experience natures deep bond.

Younger Self

Your younger self used to think she had stealth,

Playing hide and seek like no one would ever find her,

But although people did, she still wanted to continue the game,

She always used to prefer the hiding,

"It was the best part of the game",

She would say.

Your thirteen-year-old self used to struggle with her mental health,

Playing hide and seek all day long,

Only seeking at night,

Counting the time till morning,

When she'd have to do it all over again.

Now you like to seek,

Planning and preparing for the next chapter of life,

Whilst enjoying the one you're currently in,

And being kind to yourself

Creating a good life, for the girl you once were.

Conversations

Hard conversations are like rough sandpaper,

Tricky at the start before you're comfortable,

But once the edges have been worn down,

Starting to turn a light brown,

The conversations become as easy as making a mark on paper,

Your heart slowly shifting into a work of art,

The flat soil growing into a gorgeous flower,

The sandpaper becomes forgotten,

And your barriers downtrodden,

Opening the gate for constant conversation,

And contact with no expiration.

Mask

When we can't be ourselves,

We wear a mask

To hide our true feelings or personality,

And sometimes we struggle to let that go,

You may not have felt safe,

So, you didn't take the mask off

For a long time,

And now you're afraid to remove it,

Because of the judgment that you'll receive.

But once you're in a place,

Where you feel safe,

Whether it's with new people,

Or in a new place,

You can forgive yourself,

For not taking off the mask

In the past,

You can now remember,

That it's safe,

To be yourself,

You can now take off the mask.

Empty

Before healing there's a hole that needs to be filled,

Like a dried-up plant that needs revival,

Some water to bring it back to life and help its survival.

During healing the hole hasn't left yet,

The plant is still wilted,

It's in desperate need of a new filter.

The pain is leaving, yet the hole is still grieving

For something to take its place.

Afterwards, the hole has finally been filled by God,

The plant is now nourished,

It's filled with health, and rich in wealth,

All emptiness left behind,

He brought a sense of piece and wholeness.

Shame

Shame is like a rock,

As the boy is walking home, he notices some small grey rocks,

They go unnoticed by most people,

But in his content and carefree manner,

The rocks go beneath his shoes,

Causing him to slip and trip,

He felt exposed,

As passersby walked slower to watch.

He stumbled, not knowing it was once a flowing fire,

Once boiling lava, now hardened into stone,

Years ago, the thick orange lava erupted from a volcano,

It's bubbles and steams hissing as it hits the ground,

Glowing a bright crimson colour,

Liquid and flowing moving like a thick and heavy river,

Shimmering like the heat brings it to life,

Not a liquid but much more dangerous,

Burning anything, in its path.

HEALED HEART

After cooling it becomes solid and steady,

Strong and enduring, the boy is now able to handle a lot more,

It's a peaceful contrast compared to the chaos it once was.

Wind

Wind comes in sudden slow bursts,

Shaking trees and knocking over chairs,

It roars steadily, keeping its power,

More things getting devoured,

Some heavy and some light bursts start to hit,

Leaves and branches blow without falling quite low,

The soft and steady breeze keeps people at ease,

The soft blowing wind is felt softly on skin,

As it's almost faded, leaving weak gusts of air,

The air is still and peaceful,

With the memory of the wind is all that's left.

Heart

Your heart is a complicated organ,

It's the controller of the game,

It's the only part of the body that's the reason

For you being alive today,

Most of the time it chooses life over death.

In the game you try and take a step forward,

Yet the controller is lagging,

It isn't letting you move,

As much as you try,

It's useless.

You know what you need healing from,

Yet you wonder why God has kept you waiting

From taking the next step,

Sometimes your heart needs

More time to accept what your mind already knows.

Eyes

You can't see people's true feelings,

People might be good at masking,

But if you look into their eyes,

The shimmer of their irises will reveal

What they really feel.

Eyes are the only thing in a person's appearance

Which doesn't change,

You might find it hard to trust people,

But if you look into their eyes

You will see reassurance,

You will know the truth of their feelings,

A person's pupils speak volumes,

You might find it hard to trust,

But if you look into a person's eyes

You'll find the healing you've been waiting for

From the trust which you've now found.

To Younger Me

Thirteen-year-old me stood looking at herself in the mirror,

She was wearing two layered baggy tops,

I went and stood behind her,

I was wearing a fitted top, and I'm quite a bit taller than her now,

She looked at me and said, "you're so pretty",

Looking at herself and not liking what she saw,

I told her she was gorgeous how she was.

I didn't just say it to make her feel better,

I truly meant it.

To my younger self,

You're really pretty

Because everyone is beautiful in their own way,

Each person has a different type of beauty,

And there are many variations of beauty,

No version of beauty is better than another,

Nobody is prettier than you,

And you're not prettier than anyone else.

To younger me,

The world doesn't yet know your light,

And you'll glow in ways, you will soon see.

Reading

For some people reading is an outlet, something enjoyable,

For others reading is boring and a waste of time,

People who aren't a fan of reading

Will never understand the feeling of picking up a book,

And entering into a new world,

An old book's wonderful smell is something unknown to them.

The power which books have, to transform lives,

They offer knowledge and comfort,

Healing and help,

Books provide inspiration and peace,

Giving people a new perspective,

As well as unlocking emotions like empathy,

In the pages of a book,

Readers find hope and connection

This helps them navigate life's uncertainties.

Sadness

I used to believe

That sadness overwhelms creative minds.

That creativity requires sadness,

This is something I've had to unlearn and discern.

Sadness is additional to creativity,

I used to be sad all the time,

But now I've started to embrace healing

Which I've been avoiding,

And with this comes a splash of sadness.

Sadness overwhelms creative minds,

But that doesn't mean sadness is the reason for creativity.

Effort

It's hurt you,

Now it's too heavy,

And it's weighing you down,

Now it's time to leave it in this town.

You've carried it for a while,

And it's slowed you down for a long time,

You've given but never gained,

Because of the pressure and the stress

Which it's given you.

It's stolen your peace for long enough,

The past was never supposed to take up space,

Which the future should be occupying.

You should not be fearful of your future.

You need to heal the hurt which you've been hiding,

Put in the effort,

And address the core of your pain,

So that you can leave it in the past.

Leave it in that town,

And carry on travelling to the next place,

Where you will be able to rest peacefully,

Now that you've put in the effort,

To heal from your past.

Hope

Hope in the shadow of fear is the world's

most powerful motivator.

- Neal Shusterman

Unforgiveness

Unforgiveness is hard to break free from,

It's like a trapdoor which is impossible

to push open and escape,

Time and time again,

You make the same mistake,

It seems like other people

aren't struggling with this like you are,

Which makes you realise,

If Jesus could forgive Judas,

After being the reason for his death,

Why shouldn't I be able to forgive you?

I continued pushing,

Until I could finally,

Push that trapdoor,

Open and escape,

Into the freedom,

Which forgiveness gives me.

Let Go

Sometimes we have to let go,

When we are so desperately holding onto

The past, holding onto what was,

The past is like rain,

Which continues to fall over us

No matter how fast we run,

We still get wet.

We are struggling to move on,

Even though we know that moving on

is the best thing to do,

Even if we can't outrun the effect of the rain,

We can stop letting it give us more pain.

Now and again, we need to

give it to God,

Speak to him so that he can heal us,

Once in a while, we have to

Let go and let God.

Help

Time brings healing,

Is what everyone says,

But is that the truth?

Because time has passed, and I haven't healed.

But I have a friend,

Who's helping me to do so,

He's always wanted a friendship with me,

Even when I've ignored him,

Our friendship used to be on and off,

But now we've been good friends for a while,

And hopefully forever,

I learn more about him every day,

He teaches me new things all the time,

His name is Jesus Christ.

Our friendship is like a flower,

It begins to blossom,

But depending on the weather,

It may take time,

Or the process might pause,

But in the end,

We both know that it will,

Bloom once again.

Fate

Many people believe in fate,

They believe it's the reason for their existence,

For the things that happen throughout their life,

The bad and the good.

But people don't stop to wonder,

Whether it's because of someone who's in control,

Perhaps someone is putting you through those bad experiences,

And maybe someone else is blessing you.

Fate seems like a broken scale,

We beg for unknown events,

Yet we never bother wondering,

Who's causing those things to happen?

Usually, we blame God for the bad things,

Yet people never bother to thank him,

When the positives of life come along,

When we are healing,

When life finally starts getting good,

Because it's just the universe giving us a sign,

It's just fate, right?

Life

One day you'll no longer need to

Squeeze onto life so tightly,

The fear of life disappearing in between your fingers

Will be gone.

You'll slowly begin to loosen the grasp

You carefully open your palms,

Your fingers will relax their grip,

Then you'll start living life to the fullest,

Any fear which you've had in the past

Will evaporate into nothing,

You'll hold hands with healing,

And you'll enjoy the healing journey

that life takes you on.

Life is like an orange,

You continue to squeeze any opportunities,

Until there is no more juice left,

The orange peel has fallen off,

And you've finally achieved what you aimed for,

Although a few orange seeds got in your way,

You enjoyed the journey

Of healing and life.

43

Hope

The definition of hope is

A desire for something to happen,

We spend our whole lives,

Hoping for something better,

That's when we realise that it's pointless,

Hoping for something that will never occur,

We begin to feel content,

With what we currently have in our lives,

We heal from the past,

The pain that we have received,

And we start to be hopeful,

That we will no longer need to hope for anything else.

Hope is like your dream garden,

you wish it would be beautiful,

filled with flowers, trees, bees and butterflies,

But in reality, when you look out your window,

All you see is overgrown grass,

So, you decide to make your dream become the reality,

And after a few weeks or frustration as well as gratification,

You look into your garden for the second time,

And feel content,

As you've finally achieved your desired reality.

Wishing

Most people wish for things that they don't have,

They try to find a life that isn't theirs,

But they rarely succeed,

Which is why they look for that life in other places.

They begin to look for it in books,

They read and read until they find a book that fits,

That's until there are no more books left to read,

People begin to wish for more then there is,

They begin to realise that instead of wishing

They should be healing from the past.

From what made them want to feel different,

They should be wishing to heal.

Rainstorm

You can't expect to come through a rainstorm,

And find rainbows on your road,

As well as a pot of gold at your doorstep,

But you can find gold coins along the way.

Rain falls onto you

As your healing there will be good parts,

But there will be bad times too,

Because that's what healing entails,

You can't expect to find happiness

Right after a rainstorm.

Sorry

The word sorry means nothing,

Unless it's accompanied by an action,

Which shows someone is sorry.

When you're healing,

You need to stop being a people pleaser,

And accepting people's sorry

Even when you know they won't change.

Sometimes you need to be self-pleasing,

And this time you can be the one to say sorry,

Sorry for leaving, even though

They may not understand until you've left.

Because if you want to heal,

You need to self-prioritise,

Sometimes you have to say sorry,

Even to yourself.

Necklace

The process of putting together a necklace

Is hard, but it's worth it,

First you have to choose the beads,

Then you slowly place everything together,

But when the beads fall off the string,

You must put them back together once again,

It's a tedious process

But the results are beautiful.

In the same way,

Healing is hard, but it's worth it,

You find the root of the problem,

Then you have to choose to speak up about it,

Next you pray, and find out the next step

God wants you to take,

It's a hard and fearful process,

But healing is worth it.

So Long

Other people seem to have healed quickly,

You're probably feeling like it's taking

So long for you to heal,

What you don't realise is,

That other people have spent a long time

Healing and bettering themselves,

You're taking so long to heal,

Because you're doing it the right way,

Just like you should.

Healing is like a salad,

There are many different vegetables,

And multiple kinds of dressings,

As well as a few types of cheese,

Sometimes you might add potatoes too,

But in the end no matter what,

It always tastes like the angels from heaven

Have created the salad.

Hard

Sometimes we can be afraid of healing,

Because of the journey that we will take,

But when you try to go a different route,

Of not healing,

You end up desperately holding yourself together,

Which is even harder,

Because you hide your true feeling from people,

Even when they ask if you're okay,

You pretend that you are,

Even when you both know

That you're lying.

Healing is hard,

But it's definitely the best path,

In the journeys that you can take.

Light

In a dark room,

You turn on the lamp,

So that its light can shine

In the midst of the darkness,

When you're in a dark season,

And you're walking through it blindly,

Not sure where to go,

Even though the path is forwards,

But you can't see that in the dark tunnel,

Until you look around,

And see the small light

At the end of the road,

You slowly walk towards it,

And it waits for you,

You might get lost along the way,

But once you've reached the end,

You'll realise that what you've been searching for

Has been right in front of you,

Your king and saviour,

His name is Jesus Christ.

He has come to rescue you,

To give you freedom from the pain

And the suffering that you're experiencing,

He wants to heal you,

Jesus is the light in the midst of the darkness.

Leave

Often, we have to heal

From the way that people leave,

It might shock us

The sudden lack of contact.

That's what makes us realise

That if they were a true friend,

They would've stayed,

Or explained why they left,

But it gives us hope,

That God will send

Us someone who

Will never leave.

Hope is like a fire,

It burns and grows,

Many colours are shown,

Reds, yellows and oranges,

All turn into ash,

When all hope is diminished,

Because it's no longer needed,

As we've received our freedom.

Judgment

Judgment is like a tree,

It continues to grow until it is cut down,

All the squirrels and insects start to flee,

And all that's left is a tree stump which is ever so brown,

The tree bark is then turned into wood,

Its shavings scattered like dripping blood,

You continue to carve like you're building Noah's ark,

The multiple seasons and lots of strength which it takes,

As well as the worries of making mistakes,

To dodge the fear of judgment,

People's comments might make you cry,

But don't let them make you deny

The things that make you happy,

It might seem sappy,

But if people are going to judge you,

No matter what you do,

Then why would you conform to the ways of society,

People will always judge,

So why don't you let them.

Last Year

Last year may have been hard,

But giving up will make this year even harder,

Reflecting on the pain that you've been through

Instead of the paradise that you've achieved too,

Won't help you.

Don't stay in the storm,

Letting the ocean thrash against the rocks,

When sunlight is right around the corner.

Last year may have been hard,

But this year will be a year of healing,

From all the problems and pain

Which you have been put through,

And you'll gain a year of complete contentment,

Filled with sunlight and flowers,

Healing is hard,

But it's also rewarding,

Which is why this year is a year of healing,

Of joy,

And of happiness.

Disappointment

Disappointment chokes you,

Being so expectant of something,

So specific,

But then being let down.

Hands wrapping around your neck,

Yet you expect them to come loose,

But when they don't,

The feeling of defeat hits you,

Knowing you won't gain

What you so desperately yearned for.

You may feel disappointed,

Because you weren't able

To relive a moment,

Which you were only able to

live once.

Each moment you're alive,

Each second you're on this earth,

Is special, and each feeling,

Differs from the next,

Which is something you could dislike,

You may feel disappointed,

But cherish each feeling,

And remember that the next,

Will be even better than

The last.

Surviving

Surviving a storm is challenging,

But when you look back

At everything which you've achieved,

As well as the new you,

You'll find peace.

As the clouds fill up the sky,

And the thunder catches your eye,

You remember that on the other side,

There will always be light,

Going through a storm,

And coming out the other side,

Is about accepting that not every day

Will be easy, and some days

Will be hard.

It's not a race,

Everyone can go at their own pace.

Flame

Hope is like a flame in the darkness,

Once which won't go out,

As much as you try, it stays lit,

All the other peoples' flames may have extinguished,

But because you have a small amount of hope,

Your flame keeps burning,

The light which emits from your flame,

Entices everyone,

And they wonder what you have,

To keep the flicker of hope alight.

Glass

When a glass breaks,

Do you debate leaving it there?

And avoiding the area,

So that the shards don't go through

The layers of the skin on your feet.

Or do you decide to clean it up,

Even though you may get hurt,

And it will take some time,

But the result is a clean kitchen floor,

And a tidy place.

Healing takes time and effort

But the results are what makes it worth it,

Healing is scary, the first step is a big step,

And you could be fearful to start the process,

But the pretty pathway at the end of the road,

Is what makes it worth it.

Doubt

Doubt is a familiar feeling of uncertainty,

Perhaps you think this healing process will take an eternity,

Maybe you feel doubtful that it will ever end,

Before you can recommend your favourite book,

To your new friend.

When you open the book's pages,

Seeming to have experienced luck,

As you realise you've picked up a page turner,

Causing you to become a learner,

Being more informed on each character,

And the world that they live in,

As you reach the end,

You begin to question,

Where is part two?

Doubt is a feeling of uncertainty,

And if you ignore it, it'll keep going.

So, you have to stop it from endlessly flowing,

You need to realise that the process will only go on for

As long as it needs to,

Just not forever.

Existing

Sometimes you are existing to survive,

Between the heartbeats and the smiles,

Where the weight of your experiences

weights you down,

And healing hides beneath the load.

Cuts and scars cover the journey of your life,

Each step a season of hurt or healing,

The nights are an echo of silence,

And days marked with temporary sunlight.

Pain isn't the end,

But it's a step towards healing,

You are more than what's hurt you,

And the path of your healing

Will show you that.

Friendships

Friendships are like flowers,

They either grow healthily,

Or they die.

My friendship with her was the second option,

It began to grow, but then the water ran out,

A drought took place,

I tried to feed the flower, but it refused to grow,

Thankfully, my friendship with you is different,

We both water the flower, to stop it from dying out,

And so far, we are succeeding,

we don't need to feed the flower extra food,

I am glad we became friends,

You are the person I prayed about,

I feel blessed to have this friendship with you.

Arrow

The point of an arrow remembers pain,

It's sharp with all the wounds you've carried,

Left with so much to gain,

Yet it also learns to pierce the dark,

Making space for light to enter,

Opening the gate of the unexplored park.

The shaft is steady,

A spine of quiet strength,

Holding the weight of every trial,

Yet refusing to break.

The fletching whispers of direction,

Three soft wings guiding flight,

Reminding us that even when

The wind is tough; we are steadied.

The nock waits with patience,

Resting in the string of time,

Knowing release will come,

Not to destroy, but to set free.

HEALED HEART

We rise like arrows of hope,

Drawn back by hardship,

Yet sent forward by love,

Towards healing and wholeness.

Harmony

You will burn and you will burn out;
you will be healed and come back again
– Fyodor Dostoyevsky

No Revenge

No revenge,

Because one day in my teenage years,

I'll be sitting in church, midway through worship,

Deep in prayer with the Lord,

Thanking him for everything that he's given me,

I'll tell him about the amazing friendships I've been blessed with,

How grateful I am for how far he's brought me,

So happy about where I am today,

I've realised it's not too late,

Not too late to be grateful,

No matter how many months or years it's been,

Since the saddening situations,

No revenge because the way she speaks,

Reminds me of what our friendship could've been,

A friendship without arguments,

One with true happiness,

Now I have wonderful friendships,

With support and encouragement,

Without fear and the need to get out,

And no gossip involved,

No revenge,

Because silence and success are the best revenge.

Time

Time is a powerful thing,

Which we can forget.

Take some time to rest and discover,

Allowing you to recover,

From everything you've been through,

Causing you to feel blue,

You still deserve rest, which is the best.

You don't always have to be so busy,

You can pause and take a break,

Without feeling dizzy,

Take time off,

To care for yourself.

The moments of rest,

Will allow you to be blessed,

Perusing your purpose and creativity,

In everything you do,

It's good to take a break,

And it's certainly not a mistake.

Leaving

When God can see that someone isn't for me,

And he cuts down that tree,

Making that clear,

Yet I continue to pursue them,

Even though it isn't supposed to be,

He will make them hurt me,

Until I have no choice but to flee.

Leaving is like a locked door,

Being stuck inside a room which only leads to gloom,

The location of the key unknown,

And my happiness windblown.

When the door is kicked down,

And that person isn't around,

My heart will let go,

And my emotions will no longer be low.

I know that I'll be so much happier

Without them, which is true,

HEALED HEART

I am happier now then I was with you,

I needed to leave to feel free,

And now the key has been passed to me.

Revenge

I used to want you to hurt like I did,

To feel the same amount of pain and sadness,

Exactly like you made me feel,

I would've had no sympathy,

Because that's exactly what you did to me,

I used to think about all the ways I could take revenge,

To give you exactly what I thought you deserved,

But I realised that no revenge is the best revenge,

You seeing me achieve in life and heal,

Would definitely be the best revenge,

I should not try to avenge myself,

Because vengeance is the Lord's,

He is the one who will bless me and heal me,

From all the pain which you have made me suffer.

Falling

The boy thought he was falling forever,

Down the steps of struggle,

As he tried to walk back up,

He would get tripped up by bricks,

This continued to happen until what felt like forever.

That was until the person whom he viewed as his saviour,

Guided him in the right direction,

Away from the path of bricks,

He helped him all the way to the top,

And took him to a place to sit.

He healed the boys' wounds,

And his saviour listened as he spoke about his struggles,

That's when the boy realised,

He had healed in such a way,

That he fell in love, with the love of the Lord all over again.

Tidy

They say your bedroom is a reflection of your mind,

If your bedroom is a mess, what does your mind look like?

When your bed has a big pile of clothes,

Sheets sprawled all around the room,

Shoes thrown into a corner,

Your mind will barely have enough room to function,

Your grades will be plummeting into the pits of hell,

And your social life will be rapidly declining.

That's until the pile of clothes is put into the wardrobe,

The sheets are put into a folder,

And the shoes are stacked neatly,

It took time,

But your room became spotless,

And slowly, your mind cleared up,

Your grades improved and you were no longer failing,

You began to think about what you wanted your future to look like,

And you started to reconnect with your friends,

The currency of time slowed down,

It seemed like it was ending rapidly,

HEALED HEART

But it began to feel like time wasn't running away from you,

They say that your bedroom is a reflection of your mind,

Your bedroom became tidy,

And your mind was healed.

Patience

Usually people are impatient,

And as much as we like to pretend otherwise,

It is an important gift to have,

Especially when it comes to healing,

We need to learn to have the fourth fruit of the Spirit,

Because healing takes time,

And we need to be kind to ourselves,

So that we can heal healthily,

In the timing that God has for us.

Patience is important,

So that the garden of our soul

Can grow, and the flowers can bloom,

And we have to wait for the petals to show,

Otherwise, we won't see any results,

So, we need to be patient.

Beauty

People say that beauty is subjective,

Yet they act like it's an elective,

Studying styles and trends,

Like there's no end,

To the constant change,

In societies age,

What was once Visco girls,

Has been replaced by the clean girls' fake curls.

Looking through Instagram stories,

Unable to appreciate your own beauty,

You move to the back of the picture, "Excuse me".

Years pass, and trends become estranged,

Our eyes stop being trained,

To see outside beauty,

To look for a specific type of person.

Instead, we search for unique features,

Colourful eyeshadow and coils.

You begin to search in books,

Scattered search tabs and religious texts,

You start to see the truth about beauty,

And instead of "excuse me",

You start to say, "can you see me".

Because when your Creator says your beautiful,

You should believe him,

He's the creator of your beauty.

Mirror

Healing is like a mirror,

Despite the cracks and smashes,

And your hands no longer being covered in bandages,

From what you can see of your reflection,

You no longer feel the ugliness infection,

Your self-image isn't stained,

And you've stopped feeling deranged,

When people tell you you're pretty,

And you don't believe their words,

When you look to your window and see a flock of birds,

You admire their beauty,

As well as your own,

No longer feeling alone,

As you look into the mirror,

Taking your makeup off after dinner,

You feel peace at your reflection,

No longer seeing a project, but perfection

Change

Change is painful,

It's distasteful,

But staying stuck in the same place,

Will not help us to receive grace,

We must make a change,

It may feel strange,

But if you change your thoughts,

You'll stop feeling distraught,

And change will take place in your life,

It might feel as sharp as a knife,

But when you're not changing,

You're choosing to stay stuck,

In a rut,

Let's change the ending,

Healing is pending,

When the Lord blesses you,

You'll begin to think about the future too,

And you'll start to deal,

And begin to heal.

Meant to Be

Some things aren't meant to be,

We don't expect people to leave,

We just want to believe,

That we can stop being deceived,

But things can't always go our way,

Sometimes people aren't meant to stay,

We just have to pray,

For healing and believing.

Yet, other things are meant to be,

Like a newly planted tree,

Each leaf is a new stage,

As we continue to age,

We meet new people

Who see us as equals,

And go to new places,

Exposing us to new faces,

When things finally go our way,

We are able to stay,

And we realise it's meant to be.

Right

You may be afraid to take the first step

Without having any prep,

You are afraid to start your healing,

Fearing what you know will be revealing,

Which could be because,

It's not the right time to begin,

God has a timing for everything,

When the timing is right,

He will guide,

Stopping the divide in your mind,

The process will start,

When the time is right.

Acceptance

A lot of the time people struggle to accept,

And they sit in regret,

They can't believe that it has occurred,

Unable to feel secured,

So, they hold onto the past,

Not moving on fast,

And don't let go.

A tree may not want to let go of its leaves,

But it lets go and lets them fall away,

It knows that new and better things will come

Others will grow, helping life to flow,

After this season is over.

As time goes slower,

And accepting becomes courage,

While escaping suffering,

Making peace with the things

We cannot change.

Peace

There are pieces in your soul,

Which are stolen and broken,

Like a cracked token,

You might want to pretend they aren't there,

Or act like you don't care.

As the token was rolled along the floor,

After no longer being used,

And it was picked up by a new person,

Along the side of the token,

Was the word peace.

But the better option is the scariest choice,

Using your thoughts to make peace,

With your broken pieces.

Validation

The road to validation is a rough one,

We look for the validation which

we are so desperate for,

In so many things,

And we think we feel validated,

When we've found our passion,

The sensation of enthusiasm,

Which is slowly replaced by doubt.

That's when we appreciate

Finding validation on the inside,

We don't need it from other people,

Our own is enough.

Apple

The beginning of a bite into an apple,

Is hard, crispy and crunchy,

But once you reach the burst of sweetness

It's amazing.

In the same way,

Healing is hard at the start,

But once you've taken the first step,

It gets easier.

And once you've left the healing season,

You'll feel like you can breathe again,

Peace will surround you,

And gratefulness will be all you feel.

Faith Over Fear

Fear is an emotion which is rooted deep inside me,

I deeply wish for it to stop clinging to my heart,

It's like a hand which is around my heart

Continuously squeezing the life out of me,

I go out during the day and every possible issue

Which I could encounter comes into my mind,

The fear of something going wrong during my time,

Even if it's small,

The fear is still real.

Faith is the belief that I will no longer be afraid,

The hand holding my heart released its grip,

And indeed, I am free,

Now I'm able to appreciate things about my day

Rather than living a life of fear,

My life is now filled with peace and joy.

People say faith over fear,

And now I understand exactly what they mean.

The Crocus Flower

As winter subsided and spring began to unfold,

The earth still covered in cold doing as it was told,

A pop of colour broke out of its core,

The ground below cracking through the snow and still no one saw,

Came up a glistening green shoot,

Pushed by the hidden root,

Although the frost still stings people's skin,

The small beams of sun were seen as a win,

The green shoot smiles at the sun,

Realising that the cold months are almost done,

Reaching towards the warmth,

The speck of green knows it won't be alone for much longer as spring is almost here,

There is nothing more to fear,

The sun wraps along the earth,

And the crocus begins its rebirth,

A rich and healing red,

Laying in the soil bed,

Every passing pair of eyes looking as if it had been disguised,

"Spring is here" they begin to realise,

As they saw an unfamiliar flower,

Amongst the snow, like it held a strange power,

A speck of light that drew them near,

Its radiant glow formed a gentle sphere.

They called it the crocus flower.

Beauty

Beauty is pain, is a phrase that people say,

This means that your appearance is worth suffering for,

Why should the pain of beauty hurt so deep,

Like a rose without its stem,

People only see your beauty,

But what if the beauty that they see

Are the characteristics that are within,

Perhaps people have begun to look at your heart

Which they see as beautiful,

Rather than your face being a work of art.

Beauty is pain, is a phrase that people say,

Perhaps the beauty, which is spoken about,

Is the beauty within,

Maybe they realise that having both brilliance

And incredible looks,

Took effort and sacrifice,

As well as healing and lots of feelings.

Thought

When we have a thought, we believe it to be fact,

Healing begins, and we question the stories

Our minds tell us,

Fear of the future process feels absolute,

Like it defines who we are,

But the truth is these are only small moments

Not reality,

Healing comes from knowing that our thoughts

Aren't always the truth,

When we allow ourselves to stop being controlled

By our thoughts and feelings,

We begin to grow and become self-compassionate,

When we have a thought, we believe it to be fact,

We'll realise that healing isn't about erasing the past,

But about accepting where we are in the present.

Sunflower

Healing is like a sunflower that grows,

Its growth requires time,

It also takes many different seasons,

As well as weather phases,

We might need healing from something

From when we were very young,

And we grow up with that same pain,

Which honestly stung,

The stem grew taller and taller,

With leaves evolving on either side,

Then the buds began to form,

Light and bright beautiful colours,

It took some time, but they began to open,

Just as we started healing,

It takes time,

But it's worth it,

Growth and healing,

Is a specific feeling,

Which we only endure,

Once we've gone through the seasons.

Outgrow

At times we miss,

The version of people,

Which we never knew.

The person which we thought they were,

Is different from the person which

We now know.

We expected them to help us heal,

Be confident and grow,

Find our true selves,

Instead, we are with someone

Who's tearing us down,

And want us to be the worst version of ourselves.

Sometimes we outgrow people,

And that's okay.

Camera

It doesn't make sense

To call yourself ugly,

When you don't really see yourself,

You don't watch yourself sleeping,

Curled up in bed,

With your peaceful breathing rhythm.

You don't see yourself invested in a book,

Your mouth open in awe,

And your eyes glistening and glowing.

You don't see the amount of care you give to others,

The way you love your friends,

The appreciation and support you have.

There's no camera filming you,

As you laugh and smile on a day out,

When happiness is flooding out of you.

You would know exactly how beautiful you are,

If there were a camera filming the moments in your life,

And an editor to compile them into one video,

To show you exactly how much

You're truly happy knowing yourself.

Blame

Most of the time,

We blame ourselves,

For the trauma which we've been put through,

Although we know,

We shouldn't.

You know that the truth is

The only person to blame

Is the one who put you through

That situation of struggle,

Stop blaming yourself

For something which you couldn't control,

And instead begin

To heal.

Stars

There are many stars in the sky,

Each one is different,

And every star is special,

Just like there are many people on earth,

Each one is different,

Which is why you need to choose the right ones,

To help you heal, grow

And achieve,

Each person has their star,

You just need to find the right one for you.

Healed

Healing is not always light,

but rain grows flowers too

– Olivia Ann Rose

Apologise

I don't want you to apologise,

I want you to realise that you were wrong,

But sometimes the apology

Never comes when it is wanted,

And when it comes

It's neither wanted or needed.

I am the honey, and you are the bee,

Which has sucked all the life out of me,

Any potential which I once had is now being rebuilt,

The honey which used to run freely,

Has been trapped in a bottle,

But now I'm finally free from your grasp,

I don't want you to apologise,

Because I know that the sorry you say,

Would be as fake as a toy bee,

Just like you are,

I don't need you to apologise,

Because I'm thankful for what I have,

I'm happy with the people in my life,

And I'm proud of myself for protecting my peace.

Water

Having a best friend who knows everything is like water,

It has three forms: ice, steam and water, of course,

Water knows exactly what it needs to change into a different form,

Just like my best good does,

My friend has three different forms,

Jesus, the Holy Spirit and God the father,

But some people struggle to believe this,

Would you believe that water has three different forms?

Of course, you would,

So why wouldn't you believe the same thing about God.

You can't see steam, yet it still has an effect,

Just like the Holy Spirit,

He can't be seen, yet you can still feel His presence,

Jesus is like ice,

It cracks, in the same way that Jesus cracks the separation between man and God,

He gave up his life for us,

The love of Father God flows into our hearts,

Just as water flows through the streams and rivers,

And it engulfs the earth, as he heals and redeems us.

Grace

I was suffocating

Under the weight of

The things I have done in my past,

And the wrong words that I've said,

As well as the love that I didn't give.

I used to think

That it was up to me

To save myself,

But I am thankful that I know

That I was wrong,

I found out I was wrong when

I realised that the grace of God came

To save me.

He came to forgive me from my sins,

To give me freedom from the wrongdoings

Of my past,

He set me free.

LILY JOY ISAAC

God's grace grows like a flower,

He gives you His grace and forgiveness,

He forgets what you've done,

Then He takes away your pain,

He heals you from past experiences.

God's mercy and grace give you

More blessings than you could ask for.

I'm Drowning

I'm drowning,

Beneath the icy water,

Someone was pulling me deeper and deeper

Into the fast-paced ocean of pain,

I thought I'd die here,

Until the impossible happened,

His strong hand broke through the ice

Pulling me out, and wrapping me in love,

He began to heal me from all the pain,

Which I had been put through all my life.

He knew exactly what it was like,

To be betrayed, physically and mentally hurt,

He had been through more than I ever have,

He knew all the wrongs which I have done,

Yet He was still willing to save me from drowning.

Construction

I used to think I was bad at construction,

But then we built a house together,

We laid out the foundations,

Hammered in the floorboards,

And painted the walls,

Until the nails unscrewed and the paint began to chip,

But at that point we had finished building,

I tried to redo the floor space on my own,

And I ignored the peeling paint,

I thought I did a good job,

That was until the nails unscrewed once more,

I went to do the floorboards again,

But then you wanted to help me,

However, I didn't want any help.

Yet, I struggled, so I began to give up,

And you decided to help me anyway,

First you healed the cuts on my fingers,

And you tidied up the mess I had made,

Then you fixed the floorboards,

And repainted the walls.

I used to think I was bad at construction,

But then I realised that I wasn't bad at it,

When I did it with you.

Changed

I'm not the same person that I used to be,

You don't know the now-me,

The person that reads and writes to cope,

Instead of running to self-harm,

Now I have a ray of hope,

You were judgmental,

Collecting facts like it's documental,

But in the end, we all change,

The same friendships aren't exchanged,

Because at some point in my life,

I gained a new drive,

I'm a better version,

A new and improved person,

No longer the shy girl,

With yet too perfect curls,

It took time,

To create a life I can call mine,

Things happened,

And I've healed.

Flower

Bloom like a flower,

At first a flower grows,

And it's healthy,

Then it stops raining for a few days,

The petals droop,

And they begin to die,

Just like us,

We grow at first,

Mentally and physically,

Then we experience a situation,

Causing us to stop growing

And to be unhappy,

But then we begin to heal,

And just like the flower,

We bloom.

Ocean

The world is like an ocean,

When we find the part of it

That is right for us,

Breathing underwater becomes much easier,

Than when we are trying to breath

Whilst swimming next to sharks,

In the same way that in life,

If we are with the wrong people

Or in the wrong places,

It will be hard to experience life,

To the best we can,

But if we are with the right people,

Who do good things,

We will experience life to the fullest.

Life is like an ocean,

Swim with the right people,

Who will help and heal you,

HEALED HEART

If you swim with the wrong people,

They will drown you and bruise you.

Succeed

Succeeding is like wheat in the wind,

Each time someone says something

That diverts you from your dreams and passions,

Another grain flies away

And you give up on that dream,

Until the entire stalk of wheat is gone,

Then one day someone says something

Which helps you to regain your passion,

And you continue to grow your dream,

When the people who made you feel worthless

See you again,

They'll regret ever saying that

And they'll be proud of you,

If you have a dream, you can succeed.

Yellow

Yellow represents happiness,

Evacuating any nastiness,

It represents the small ray of sunshine

Not allowing any feelings to decline,

Which is in your life when you're in pain,

And you have so much to gain,

As your healing,

Denied emotions start revealing,

The spot of yellow expands

Ignoring unwanted commands,

Into a yellow blob of paint,

Removing all restraints,

Until your entire page is painted in yellow,

And before you've realised what's happened,

You notice that you've healed.

Happen

When we are healing

We will go through many feelings,

Questioning why something has happened,

Our emotions no longer seeming saddened,

And wondering why God let us go through it,

Why did our heart get slit?

But a lot of the time we forget,

Causing us to regret,

All the times we questioned,

God's timing and his reasoning,

Remembering something that we aren't able to understand,

As Satan expresses his reprimand.

God's ways are higher than our ways,

We should try our best to obey,

Knowing everything will be okay one day,

He knows that it had to happen,

And that we will regain our passion,

So, we could grow,

All explanations will be revealed,

Eventually we will heal.

Happier

People tell the girl that she looks happier,

She says thank you,

Telling them it was God.

They don't think anything of it,

But what they don't realise,

Is everything she has been through,

The pain and problems,

Every night vacuumed of sleep,

Filled with thoughts, dreaded and deep.

Each thing that God has healed her from,

The journey that she has been taken on,

It's thanks to God that she is happier now.

Freedom

There are many things in life,

We wish we had control of,

But these things

Are out of our hands.

And our minds,

Deserve freedom from them too.

The not-so-far-away reach for freedom

Is like digging into the sand to reach the water,

You can see the water, but you can't feel it,

Beneath your fingertips Is the sea's extension,

And in reality, you're begging for perfection.

The Lord can give us freedom

From these things,

He can give us healing and peace,

You deserve freedom,

From the pain that freely reigns,

With no exit,

In your mind.

Stronger

People say that struggle makes you stronger,

Which is a phrase which is quite controversial,

And many people disagree,

Because the true meaning

Is hidden beyond the surface of a word,

The real and right meaning

Of this phrase is,

It's the healing after your struggle,

That makes you stronger.

Healing makes you stronger,

It helps you to realise and know

Your own strength,

Now that you've survived something

Which seems impossible,

Now you are empowered,

As well as encouraged

To survive anything.

And other people won't realise this,

HEALED HEART

Healing has made you stronger,

Because you've gone through things,

That other people

Will never understand,

Or ever know.

Joy

You hear the word joy,

Not truly knowing what it means,

In the pain and the suffering

That you're journeying through,

You crave to feel the unknown,

And you expect to never sit

In this heavenly feeling

For the entirety of your life,

But you're wrong,

And what you're forgetting,

Is that once you've healed,

From the pain that you

Were once put through,

You will be able to dance in the joy

That you have been desiring.

Speak Up

The girl feels silenced,

Even though no one has silenced her

Or oppressed her opinions.

All her life she has been an echo

Of other peoples' beliefs,

She has merely repeated the views

That she agrees with.

But now it's her time

To be a voice,

Not an echo.

It's her turn to speak up,

She became the first

To give her opinion,

Instead of the last.

To agree with the view of others,

Now the sound of her voice,

And the glow of her eyes,

Makes people want to speak up,

She heals people with her words

Which are from heaven,

She was unsilenced,

She spoke up.

Hurt

Most of the time

Healing will hurt and hurt,

Until eventually, the pain

Will cease to exist.

You'll look back on memories

Which you shared,

And you'll wish

You were still together,

That's until you remember,

All the terrible times which

You experienced together,

And you'll know

That parting ways was the best option,

It might be painful now,

But long term you know

That staying together would've

Hurt you more than

Breaking up did.

Intentions

Be intentional about healing,

Don't go back to the things that hurt you,

Take time in your healing season,

Take hold of the root of your pain,

And forcefully pull it out,

Uproot the problem,

And never replant it.

This takes time,

Perhaps you'll slowly cut off sections

Until you reach the root,

And remove the main source.

Be intentional about healing,

And give yourself time

To fully heal.

Full Stop

When a pen places the last drop of ink on the paper,

The full stop, the end of the sentence

Chapter or paragraph,

Is when I realised that I hate endings,

I hate ends of books,

Car rides and good times.

The good things about endings,

Is, they're a signal for new beginnings,

Endings are an opportunity to make a change,

To start a fresh page.

The pen lifts from the page,

And the full stop is there,

But I no longer hate endings,

The next chapter of my life is about to begin,

The full stop is a sign of a new season of life.

Words

It's strange,

You know yourself better

Then anyone else knows you,

Yet you cry and crumble,

At the words of someone different,

Who hasn't even lived a second

Of life from your perspective.

They haven't had your experiences,

Or been in any of the same situations,

You need to focus on your own voice,

Opinions, words and views,

It's the only thing that truly matters.

Thread

We experience suffering in quiet ways,

A few comments and an experience,

Life hanging on at the end of a thread,

Until it comes undone,

Healing is like a thread,

It's thin and flimsy at first,

Unravelling at the ends,

Fraying at the edges as it comes apart,

It doesn't improve its condition quickly,

The stitches slowly come back together,

Twist and untangle,

Each pull brings us closer.

When the string of thread has been mended,

We aren't the same as we it used to be,

With a new pattern,

Travelling up the twists and turns

Of the material,

Softer in the middle,

And stronger at the ends,

Healed overall.

Blue

The colour blue usually represents sadness,

But what if it could represent healing,

The sea is known to be blue,

It engulfs the grains of sand into its midst,

And it spits out different types of grains,

Onto the shore.

The same way that when we heal,

We discover new parts of ourselves,

And of our past which we are healing from

Stay hidden away.

Healing is blue,

Just like the sea.

Healed Heart

There was a hole in my heart,

It's been stitched back together,

I used to feel anger and sadness,

Now I feel joy and peace,

In what was once a garden

Filled with dead plants,

Flowers are now growing,

And new plants are budding,

It's taken me too long to realise,

That healing might take time,

It's a long process,

To heal from the painful parts of life,

But now I feel peace,

What was once broken,

Has now been healed.

Safe

People begin to heal in places

Where they feel safe and seen,

When someone genuinely says with kindness,

That they understand and are willing to listen,

People heal in spaces where judgment

Is void and non-existent,

Where arms are open with compassion

As well as care,

Where shame can be subsided and stripped,

Where light erupts over darkness,

Where love is everlasting,

Healing happens here.

Cars

Calm car drives, give us peace,

A car never stays in the same place

When it's on the road,

It's always moving whether

It's slow or fast.

You are always healing,

Whether it's happening quickly

Or not,

You're still healing.

Life moves on like a car,

Healing takes place,

And memories are made,

We heal and we change.

Acknowledgements

Thank you to my friends and family for encouraging me and helping me through the process of writing this poetry book. I am so grateful to have these amazing people in my life, and I feel so blessed by God to have these friendships. Of course, I would also like to thank Jesus for giving me the talent to write these poems and for the healing journey which he is currently taking me on. Lastly, thank you to my readers for making me able to publish this book and achieve my dreams.

Starting a healing journey, whether it's with or without God, is a scary thing, but with the goodness of God and the people around us for support, I know that we can all get through this.

Whether you believe in God or not, I want you to know that He truly does love you and cares for you. You might be wondering how that's true if there's so much suffering in the world. But take the story of Job in the Bible for example, this story is in the book of Job in the Old Testament, it's the 18th book in the bible. Job was a righteous mas who was fulfilled in the life he had, God Who provided him with family, friends, and everything else that he needed. But his faith was tested by his suffering, Satan challenged God, claiming that Job only follow's him because he had succeeded so far in life. To test Job's faith, God allows Satan to take away his wealth, health family and friends. Despite Job's extreme amount of suffering, he continues to be faithful to God, although he questions why he is suffering. His friends begin to insist that this is a punishment and that he has sinned, but Job maintains his belief in the Lord. After the time of suffering, God restores Job's loss and gives him double of everything which he had, blessing him even more than before. God reminds Job that as humans we won't always understand Gods plans, and we should continue to trust in him no matter the circumstances.

Job went through so much suffering in his life, he lost everything, his family, friends and belongings. Yet God only let him go through that because he knew that Job would be able to do that. God doesn't let us experience struggle or suffering if he knows that we won't be able to handle it. At the end of Job's story God gave back to him double what Satan had taken from him. So, no matter what you're going through and what you feel like you're losing, God will always provide so much more for you in the future.

I want to share my story of how God has helped me in my life; I would appreciate it if you could have a read of my experience.

My Testimony

I grew up in a Christian household. We went to church every Sunday, and I read the bible occasionally, but I never knew Jesus on a personal level. When I was fourteen, my mental health began to suffer, and I felt unmotivated towards everything in life. I had no idea what my purpose was, and I hid how I felt from everyone. I began to seek temporary relief from these burdens, which is when I began to self-harm. There was a time when it got so bad that it was a daily addiction. Throughout this time, I still believed in God, but I was not seeking him, and I had no idea what to do. I told my friend Rachael about how I felt, and she helped me as best she could. When my mum found out about it, she was upset for me, and I knew she had been praying for me to have freedom from my struggles. Maybe you've heard similar stories to this before, about how God has helped people who have had bad mental health, but that wasn't all. At the same time as this, I delt with judgment about past choices.

At the time, the youth group where I attended were going for a few days away for a conference. On the first evening meeting, the person speaking said that she knew that someone in the room had self-harm scars. Only my friend Rachael knew about this, and I trusted that she didn't tell this youth leader about my self-harm. In this moment, I knew that God was the one who told her this. Later that night, this same youth leader sat with me, she told me that I had a wall that I needed to name so I could break it down. I knew that this wall was self-harm, and my struggles with mental health as a whole. Later in the conference, I had a conversation with this youth leader again, and I figured out God had also told her that I delt with judgment about past choices, and that this was not wrong.

A day later, God had revealed to me that I was like a pigeon. This confused me at first, but I discovered pigeons always return to their original homes. I thought I would go to hell, but this was God telling me that I would return to him in heaven when my time came.

A few months after this, I began to rebuild my relationship with Christ, and I was set free from bad mental health. I got baptised on the same day as Rachael. The heavenly and joyful feeling that came over me when I was in the baptism pool was honestly beautiful and I've never experienced anything like it.

However, about a year afterwards, there was a short period of time, about a week, where I felt my bad mental health coming back again. I refused to give into temptation to self harm and the urge to relapse. Instead, what I began to do was to read my bible as soon as I woke up, and to listen to worship music before I went to sleep (or whenever I felt down). This has been a great method in my healing journey.

I am so grateful for how far the Lord has brought me through my journey of faith and in life, and I still am continuing to go through my healing journey. This is hard, but I know that I will come out on the other side much more joyful than how I entered, instead of getting the temporary feeling of happiness from things that are only temporary.

Hard times can still come even after the deliverance from God, but he will always take you through them. These experiences helped me learn how to deal with them better each time. I learn new skills on every bump in my journey, which helps make the recovery process faster.

My sadness has showed me that I need saving. I now appreciate the beauty of life, and I value myself more than ever because I know that my worth comes from Jesus. I pray that God can help you to do the same, and I hope my testimony shows that God can do the same for you. God bless you!

"The Lord bless you and keep you; the Lord make his face shine on you and be gracious to you; the Lord turn his face toward you and give you peace."

– Numbers 6:24-26

About the Author

Lily Isaac is a teen poet and author based in England. Of Egyptian heritage and Arabic descent, she brings a unique cultural and emotional lens to her writing. Her journey into poetry began during a deeply challenging time in her life, when words became a refuge and a way to process pain, fear, and identity struggles. What started as a coping mechanism evolved into a powerful creative outlet, and ultimately, a voice for others who feel like they might not be able to achieve healing.

Her work is rooted in lived experience; her writing became a way to express her happiness and healing journey. Through her poetry, she aims to remind readers that they are not alone, that their emotions are valid, and that connection can be found even in the darkest moments.

This collection is a testament to resilience, vulnerability, and the healing power of expression. Lily writes not to impress, but to offer comfort, solidarity, and hope to anyone who needs it.